ISAAC ASIMOV'S NEW LIBRARY OF THE UNIVERSE

POLLUTION IN SPACE

BY ISAAC ASIMOV
WITH REVISIONS AND UPDATING BY GREG WALZ-CHOJNACKI

Gareth Stevens Publishing
MILWAUKEE

For a free color catalog describing Gareth Stevens' list of high-quality books, call 1-800-542-2595 (USA) or 1-800-461-9120 (Canada). Gareth Stevens' Fax: (414) 225-0377.

Mr. Walz-Chojnacki gratefully acknowledges Mr. Bernard Kelm of AlliedSignal Technical Services Corporation for his assistance with the preparation of this edition.

Library of Congress Cataloging-in-Publication Data

Asimov, Isaac.
  Pollution in space / by Isaac Asimov ; with revisions and
updating by Greg Walz-Chojnacki.
    p. cm. — (Isaac Asimov's New library of the universe)
  Rev. ed. of: Space garbage. 1989.
  Includes bibliographical references and index.
  ISBN 0-8368-1196-8
  1. Space debris—Juvenile literature. [1. Space debris.]
  I. Walz-Chojnacki, Greg, 1954-. II. Asimov, Isaac. Space garbage.
  III. Title. IV. Series: Asimov, Isaac. New library of the universe.
  TL1499.A85 1995
  363.72'8'0919—dc20   94-32485

This edition first published in 1995 by
Gareth Stevens Publishing
1555 North RiverCenter Drive, Suite 201
Milwaukee, Wisconsin 53212, USA

Project editor: Barbara J. Behm
Design adaptation: Helene Feider
Editorial assistant: Diane Laska
Production director: Susan Ashley
Picture research: Kathy Keller
Artwork commissioning: Kathy Keller and Laurie Shock

Printed in the United States of America

1 2 3 4 5 6 7 8 9 99 98 97 96 95

To bring this classic of young people's information up to date, the editors at Gareth Stevens Publishing have selected two noted science authors, Greg Walz-Chojnacki and Francis Reddy. Walz-Chojnacki and Reddy coauthored the recent book *Celestial Delights: The Best Astronomical Events Through 2001.*

Walz-Chojnacki is also the author of the book *Comet: The Story Behind Halley's Comet* and various articles about the space program. He was an editor of *Odyssey*, an astronomy and space technology magazine for young people, for eleven years.

Reddy is the author of nine books, including *Halley's Comet, Children's Atlas of the Universe, Children's Atlas of Earth Through Time*, and *Children's Atlas of Native Americans*, plus numerous articles. He was an editor of *Astronomy* magazine for several years.

CONTENTS

We live in an enormously large place – the Universe. It's just in the last fifty-five years or so that we've found out how large it probably is. It's only natural that we would want to understand the place in which we live, so scientists have developed instruments – such as radio telescopes, satellites, probes, and many more – that have told us far more about the Universe than could possibly be imagined.

We have seen planets up close. We have learned about quasars and pulsars, black holes, and supernovas. We have gathered amazing data about how the Universe may have come into being and how it may end. Nothing could be more astonishing.

We have explored many areas of our Solar System, especially the regions close to Earth. We have sent numerous rockets into space, most of which continue to orbit Earth even after they stop working. The result is that nearby outer space is filled with space debris – or space pollution. In this book, we will take a look at pollution in space and discover why scientists are concerned.

Isaac Asimov

A Junkyard in Space

Satellites have been placed in orbit around Earth since the late 1950s. Most of these satellites are still circling our planet, even though many of them are no longer working. Some old satellites have broken apart. There are also bits of rockets that stayed in space after their original jobs were completed. There are now more than 25,000 pieces of space debris at least the size of a sugar cube circling Earth.

Fortunately, there is a lot of room in space. But as more and more satellites and other spacecraft are put into orbit, the problem of pollution in space gets bigger.

Left: Satellites and orbital debris are swarming around Earth today in record numbers.

Below: Beyond the debris clustered close to Earth are thin rings of debris that orbit Earth farther out in space.

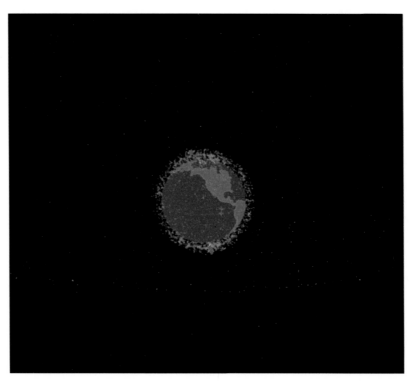

Divide and Multiply

One big problem with space debris is that it can multiply. When a piece of debris is broken apart in a collision with another piece of space junk, its pieces can start colliding with each other. Where there were two objects, soon there are hundreds more!

Another problem is that space debris moves very fast – thousands of miles (kilometers) per hour – and with great force. In space, a piece of aluminum the size of a sugar cube can hit with the force of a 400-pound (180-kilogram) safe moving at 60 miles (97 km) per hour!

If we don't put an end to pollution in space, we'll end up with a space environment where there are constant collisions creating ever more debris – and then more collisions!

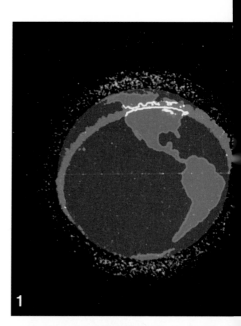

1

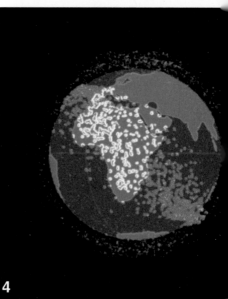

4

! Lunar litter – the last trace of humanity?

Suppose that a nuclear war wipes out all of humanity. Gradually, wind, water, and any remaining forms of life then destroy what is left of our cities. If visitors from some other civilization come to Earth millions of years later, they may find no sign that humans ever existed. But on the Moon, there would still be the litter our astronauts left behind between 1969 and 1972, looking almost as it did originally.

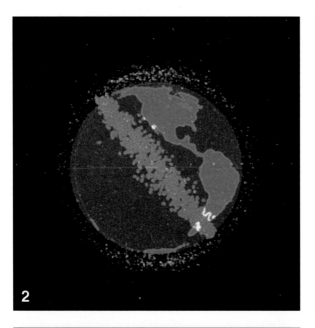

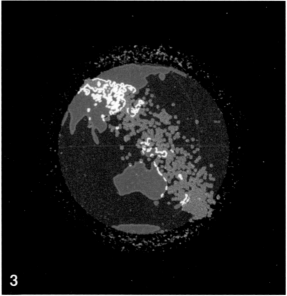

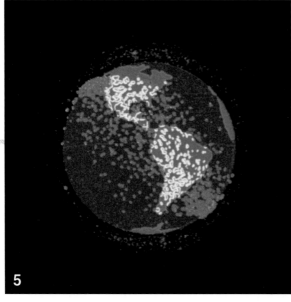

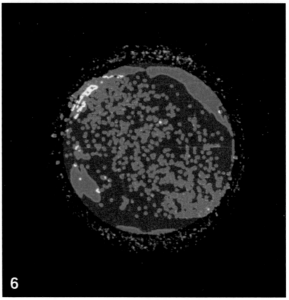

Above: Scientists studying the debris orbiting Earth used a computer to show how a piece of space junk gradually turns into a cloud of dangerous debris.

Running Out of Outer Space

Space debris is not just a matter of messiness. It is important to know where it is, especially the big pieces. After all, if we send additional satellites into space, we don't want to put them into an orbit where they will collide with a piece of debris and be destroyed. One reason we send radio waves into space is to track space trash.

Radio waves bounce off satellites and debris, giving scientists on Earth the exact location of each object in space (whether working or dead) and where each object is headed. This helps determine a good orbit for the next satellite.

But one day soon, we just may run out of safe orbits!

Opposite: Radar dishes such as these are part of a worldwide electronic "trash-tracking" network designed to locate debris in outer space.

Bottom, left: From an underground post beneath Cheyenne Mountain in Colorado, scientists at the United States Space Surveillance Center keep track of about seven thousand pieces of space debris.

Bottom, right: For several nights following the launch of *Skylab* in 1973, several "extra" satellites streaked across the night sky. They were parts of the rocket that launched the huge space laboratory.

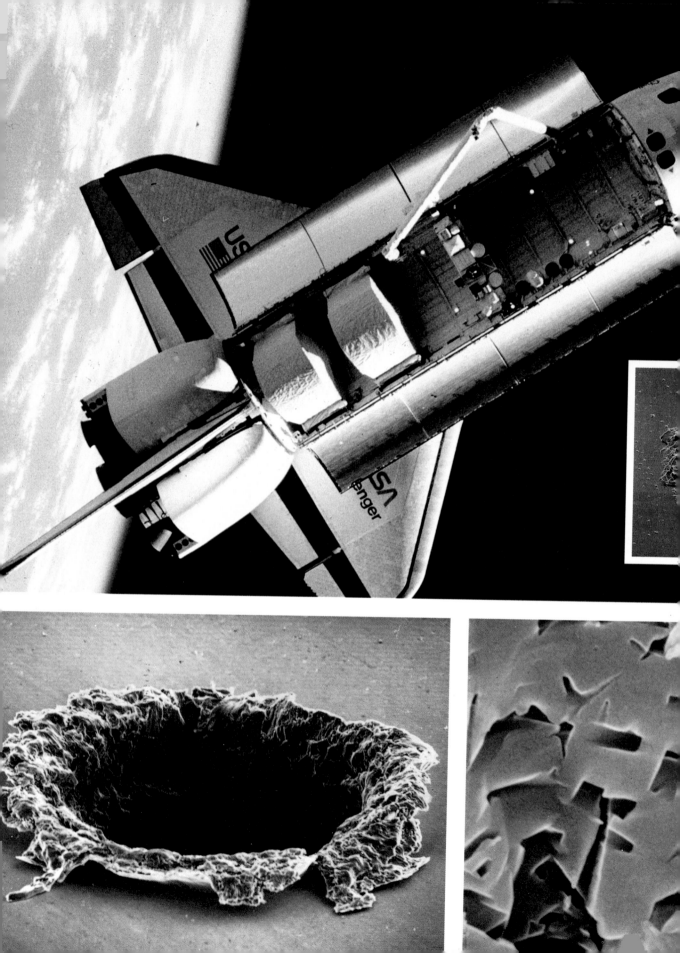

Tiny, but Deadly, Dangers

Space contains numerous meteoroids, most of which are the size of a grain of sand. But they move at many miles (km) a second, and even a small one can puncture a space suit and kill an astronaut. Fortunately, space is vast, and so far no "killer meteoroid" has struck an astronaut.

Space debris is equally dangerous. A fleck of paint struck a space shuttle in 1983 and chipped the windshield, which had to be replaced at a cost of $50,000. A slightly larger object might have punctured the windshield and caused the deaths of the astronauts on board.

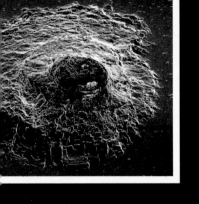

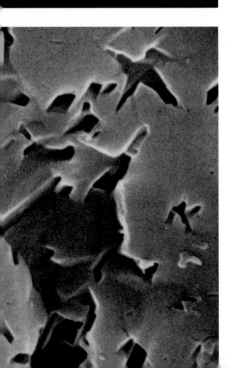

Top: A tiny fleck of paint chipped and made a tiny crater *(inset)* in the windshield of the U.S. space shuttle *Challenger.*

Opposite, bottom, left: Many tiny craters like this (in a magnified view) were found on the *Solar Maximum* satellite after its return to Earth in 1984. High-speed flakes of paint did the damage.

Left: Particles streaming from the Sun leave their marks (magnified) on Moon rocks. However, Earth's atmosphere deflects most of these particles.

! Solar wind – another kind of debris

The Sun is constantly hurling out its own "debris"– electrically charged particles – called the solar wind. This radiation is harmful but not enough to threaten astronauts. However, occasionally there is an explosion on the Sun called a solar flare. Then the number of these particles rises to a deadly level. There was an enormous solar flare in 1972 at an interval between the two Moon missions. Luckily, there were no astronauts in space at the time.

11

The Space Station – A Big Target

The dangers may be great for the new International Space Station to have a collision with space debris. When completed, the space station will be quite large, and it will be in orbit for ten years or more. It will be 361 feet (110 meters) long and 293 feet (89 m) across – a big target. Scientists are working hard to determine how likely it is that the space station will be struck by a piece of space junk.

To protect the astronauts on board, the station will have special shielding to keep debris from penetrating. Also, there will be many airtight compartments. If one compartment is punctured, the crew will be able to seal it off and go to other, safer quarters.

Opposite: The International Space Station, a joint project between the United States, Europe, Canada, Japan, and Russia, will be an orbiting laboratory housing six astronauts. Scientists are concerned that its size makes the space station a dangerously big target for space debris.

Left: The International Space Station's compartments can be sealed off from one another. If one compartment is damaged, astronauts can move to another for safety.

13

Satellites – Can't Live Without Them

From the time satellites were first launched into space in the 1950s, the human race has come to depend on information sent back to Earth by the satellites. For instance, some of the satellites help predict the weather and track storms.

In addition, some satellites make it possible for people to send messages across the oceans. Other satellites allow sailors to know the exact location of their ships at all times. Still other satellites make it possible for scientists to study Earth – its soil, its oceans, and its crops.

We have come to depend on satellites. But as long as we continue to use them, we will continue to end up with space pollution.

Left: Hurricane Juan was tracked by a weather-watching satellite *(inset).*

Below, left: Europe's Infrared Space Observatory, or ISO, measures the heat of newborn stars.

Below, right: This orbiting "crystal ball," *LAGEOS* (Laser Geodynamic Satellite), may one day help predict earthquakes. Scientists bounce laser beams off its hundreds of reflectors in order to measure movements in Earth's crust.

The Sky Is Falling

Space debris can even be dangerous to living things on Earth. Debris can pass through thin wisps of Earth's upper air and gradually come close to Earth, entering the main atmosphere. Small pieces just burn up. But large pieces can reach Earth's surface. Nearly three-quarters of these pieces will splash into the ocean, but some may hit land. Parts of a satellite, *Cosmos 954*, from the former Soviet Union, fell on northern Canada in 1978.

Also in 1978, increased activity on the surface of the Sun heated Earth's atmosphere, causing it to expand. This increased the atmosphere's "drag" on the U.S. *Skylab* satellite, until parts of *Skylab* finally came down in western Australia the following year. It's not very likely that pieces of satellites will hit buildings or people because most of Earth is covered with water. But someday a lump of debris may do just that.

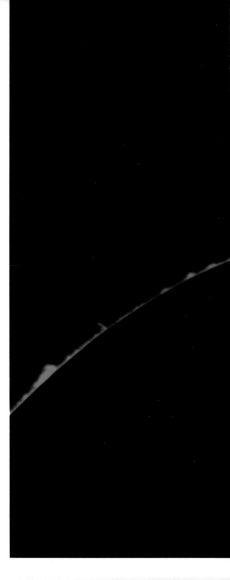

Top: A plume of gas rises above the Sun's surface. This kind of activity can expand Earth's atmosphere and drag satellites into low orbits.

Bottom, left: When the satellite, *Cosmos 954*, fell to Earth, it scattered radioactive debris that had to be located and safely removed.

Opposite, bottom, right: Pictured is part of a water tank recovered when *Skylab* broke apart in Earth's atmosphere.

16

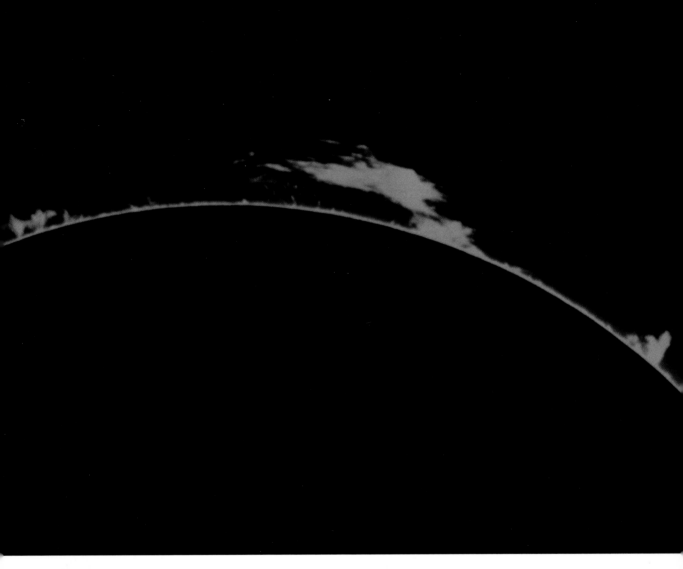

What Are the Chances?

About 30 percent of Earth's surface is land, and only about 1 percent of this land has large concentrations of people on it. So if a large piece of debris falls to Earth, the chances are only about 1 in 333 that it might strike land and do serious harm to human beings. This means that if a large piece of space debris falls to Earth only once every 10 years, then the odds are that it will be some 3,000 years or more before a piece causes serious harm to people on Earth.

Of course, by bad luck, a piece might hit next year. As our planet's population increases daily and cities spread outward, the chances for harm also increase. On the other hand, if we start cleaning up outer space, the chances for harm will decrease.

Opposite: The *Skylab Orbiting Workshop* was launched by the United States in 1973. Pieces of it fell to Earth in 1979.

Below, left: Satellites that fall to Earth burn and break apart in Earth's atmosphere.

Below, right: The bright plume of a solar flare leaps above the Sun's surface.

? *Solar flares – life-and-death questions remain.*

Explosions on the Sun that expel a deadly tide of charged particles take place at odd times. Scientists don't always know what causes these solar flares or when they'll take place. This means that astronauts working at a space station, for instance, will never know when to expect these dangerous events – so the station will have to be shielded at all times. After further future study, flares may someday become predictable, and life in space will be safer.

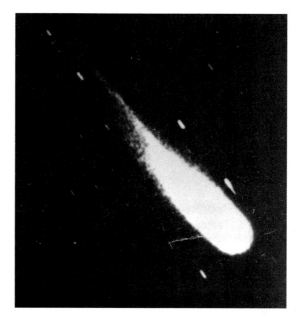

18

Top: In this illustration, a half-buried *Viking* lander on Mars shows its age after centuries of erosion.

Right: A robot explorer on Mars awaits an oncoming dust storm.

Far right: The Russian probe *Venera* rests on the surface of Venus. The probe stopped transmitting an hour after it landed – its electronics destroyed by the planet's tremendous heat.

To Be or Not To Be? – Space Pollution

Much of the debris in nearby outer space will return harmlessly to Earth. In this way, nearby space could be called "self-cleaning." Farther from Earth, space also cleans up after itself much of the time. The probes that have landed on Venus will be exposed to very high temperatures and strong winds, and they will eventually turn to dust. On Mars, sandstorms might do the same to the debris, only more slowly.

But on places like our Moon and Phobos (a moon of Mars), there is no atmosphere to wear down any litter. On these worlds, debris left behind could last for millions of years. So it is important to remember that under some conditions, our junk may be around forever.

Of course, if we set up a permanent lunar base, we can at least keep the Moon clean. But what about the other litter we leave in the cosmos? It will all add up!

? Cosmic rays – the debris of a dying star?

Cosmic ray particles are more penetrating and deadly than solar wind particles. But usually there are not enough of them to be dangerous. Astronomers think cosmic ray particles originate with supernovas, or violently exploding stars. A nearby supernova may make space deadly for a time. Stars do not explode as supernovas often, and only a few stars are close enough to be dangerous! But it's hard to predict when a supernova explosion will take place.

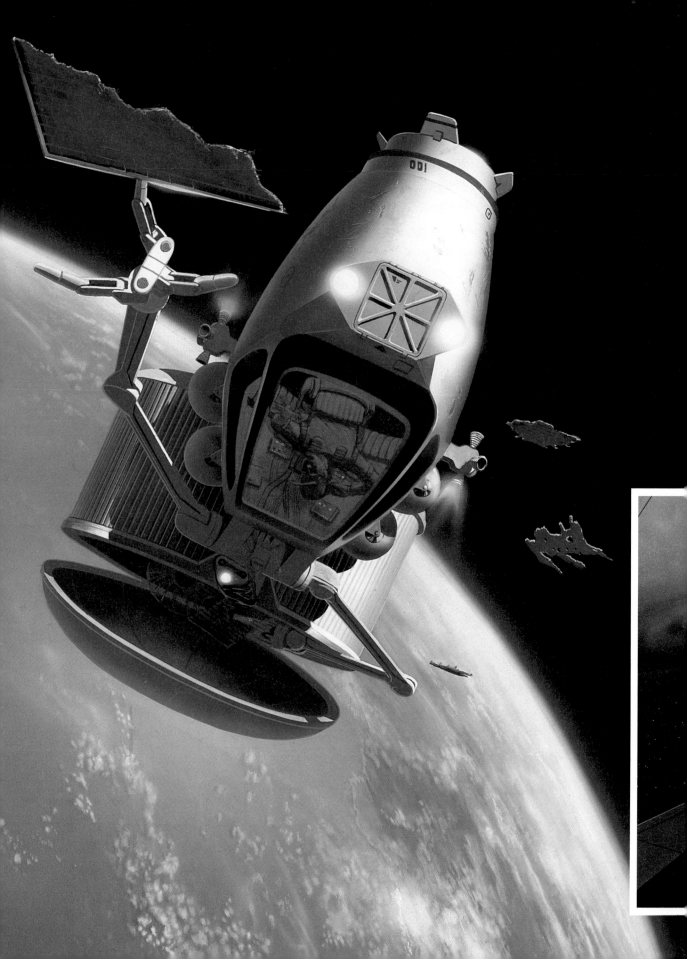

Cleaning Up and Preventing Pollution in Space

If too much debris accumulates around Earth, it might become impossible for scientists to find safe orbits for future satellites. One of the tasks of some space shuttle missions is to pick up satellites that aren't working and repair them or remove them from space.

Researchers now have the task of developing satellites that don't easily break apart and that survive collisions with debris. Someday there may even be a way to sweep up the debris.

So far, nothing much has been done to clean up pollution in space. If we continue to do nothing, increasing amounts of debris could put an end to space exploration once and for all.

Opposite: Low orbits are the most littered with space debris. Perhaps one day orbiting "garbage collectors" will be used to clean up these trash-filled orbits.

Left: Black holes may one day be the ultimate trash-mashers. Advanced civilizations may use black holes to dispose of their space garbage.

On an Endless Journey

In 1957, scientists launched *Sputnik 1*, Earth's first artificial satellite. More recently, space probes have been sent beyond the planets. The *Pioneer 10* probe is now moving far beyond the known Solar System and is still sending back messages. It could do so until after the year 2000, but eventually it will stop working. Then, it will continue moving outward as a far-flung piece of junk.

Other probes will follow, and one day there might be large numbers of such dead objects sailing through interstellar space for countless millions of years. Of what value will these objects be during their endless journey into the cosmos?

! *Skimming the stars*

Where are the deep-space probes headed? One of them, Voyager 2, *continues to move outward after taking pictures of Uranus in 1986 and of Neptune in 1989. In about forty thousand years, it will skim by a red dwarf star named Ross 248 and be only 1.65 light-years away from it. That's still almost 10 trillion miles (16 trillion km) away – not very close! But it's the closest* Voyager 2 *will come to any star other than our Sun in the first million years of its journey.*

Opposite: Earth's deep-space probes sail beyond the outer reaches of our Solar System. This artist's conception shows *Voyager 2 (foreground)*, with *Pioneers 10 and 11* off to the right. Also shown *(background)* is the path of *Voyager 1*, which passed through the plane of Saturn's rings at a steep angle and headed up and away from the Solar System.

The "Strange" Planet Earth

Some deep-space probes carry with them plaques giving information about Earth and its location. Some carry audio recordings with various sounds on them, including music and the voices of humans speaking. The idea behind this is that someday – perhaps millions of years from now – intelligent beings from other worlds may come across such distant debris and discover the plaques and recordings.

Will it be dangerous to attract the attention of aliens? Probably not; there's no reason to think that intelligent beings from distant planets would be unfriendly.

Perhaps even human beings millions of years from now living in distant space may discover the plaques and recordings. Will they be able to understand the information sent out so long ago? Or will they be so distant from Earth in time and space that they will wonder how beings so much like them could have lived on such a "strange" planet like Earth?

Opposite: The time is 100 million years from now. The place is somewhere in interstellar space. *Voyager 2* is now just a nonworking craft floating in space in the area of a red supergiant star. The craft is covered with tiny craters caused by the impact of countless meteoroids.

Right, top: A plaque aboard *LAGEOS* (see photo, page 15) shows three views of Earth's shifting continents: one of the distant past, one of the present, and one of the distant future.

Right, bottom: A plaque aboard *Pioneer 10* includes images of a man and a woman. The man's hand is raised in a sign of goodwill. A diagram of the Solar System pictures *Pioneer 10* leaving Earth, flying by Mars and Jupiter, and sailing into interstellar space.

Fact File:
Space Pollution – Good and Bad

Like many other things, much of what we send into space – or what comes our way from space – can be good or bad. Satellites can help warn us about dangerous storms, but they can also be dangerous themselves when their debris falls to Earth. In the same way, objects in space, such as meteorites, might cause damage on Earth if they fall in the wrong place. But they can also help us learn more about the Universe. Here are some benefits and drawbacks of various objects in space.

Opposite: Artists' depictions of various objects that may lead to pollution in space (*clockwise, from top):* satellites intercept nuclear warheads; spacecraft sail through space powered by the Sun; a meteoroid hits Earth's atmosphere; workers in outer space mine the asteroids.

Type of "Space Pollution"	Good Points	Bad Points
Meteoroids, meteorites, and asteroids	May contain substances that help us learn more about the Universe and the origin of life as we know it	May be dangerous if they hit Earth's surface or piloted spacecraft
Piloted spacecraft	Enable humans to explore space first-hand, repair satellites or return them to Earth if they are in danger of falling; first step to human colonies in space	Space travel still extremely expensive and dangerous; larger craft orbiting Earth, like *Skylab*, can be dangerous when they fall out of orbit
Satellites	Vital for purposes of navigation, modern communication, weather forecasting, national defense, and space exploration	Expensive; can malfunction; increasing number of satellites increases problems and dangers of pollution in space
Solar wind and solar flares	Possible future source of energy for Earth and for propelling future spacecraft	Danger to space travelers; danger to humans on Earth if damage to atmosphere continues; disruptive to Earth communications
Unpiloted space probes (Hubble Space Telescope, *Pioneer*, *Mariner*, *Voyager*, etc.)	Safe way of exploring and learning about the Universe; can go places no human can safely go, such as the surface of Venus and the outer Solar System and beyond; can help scientists learn things about space they could not learn from a base on Earth	Individual probes can be expensive and take a long time to develop; debris from launch rockets can cause pollution in space; probes take a long time to travel to their destination and begin the transmission of data

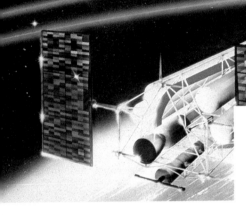

More Books about Pollution in Space

Artificial Satellites. Bendick (Franklin Watts)
Comets and Meteors. Couper (Franklin Watts)
Comets, Meteors and Asteroids: Rocks in Space. Darling (Dillon)
Cosmic Debris: The Asteroids. Asimov (Gareth Stevens)
Discovering Comets and Meteors. Asimov (Gareth Stevens)
Exploring Outer Space: Rockets, Probes, and Satellites. Asimov (Gareth Stevens)
Our Planetary System. Asimov (Gareth Stevens)
Voyager: The Story of a Space Mission. Poynter and Lane (Atheneum)

Videos

The Asteroids. (Gareth Stevens)
Comets and Meteors. (Gareth Stevens)

Places to Visit

You can explore outer space – including the places close to our planet where space pollution is becoming more and more of a problem – without leaving Earth. Here are some museums and centers where you can find a variety of space exhibits.

NASA Lyndon B. Johnson Space Center
2101 NASA Road One
Houston, TX 77058

Australian Museum
6-8 College Street
Sydney, NSW 2000 Australia

San Diego Aero-Space Museum
2001 Pan American Plaza - Balboa Park
San Diego, CA 92101

National Air and Space Museum-Smithsonian
Seventh and Independence Avenue SW
Washington, D.C. 20560

Edmonton Space and Science Centre
11211 - 142nd Street
Edmonton, Alberta T5M 4A1

The Space and Rocket Center and Space Camp
One Tranquility Base
Huntsville, AL 35807

Places to Write

Here are some places you can write for more information about our Universe, including pollution in space. Be sure to state what kind of information you would like. Include your full name and address so they can write back to you.

National Space Society
922 Pennsylvania Avenue SE
Washington, D.C. 20003

Jet Propulsion Laboratory
Teacher Resource Center
4800 Oak Grove Drive
Pasadena, CA 91109

Sydney Observatory
P. O. Box K346
Haymarket 2000 Australia

Canadian Space Agency
Communications Department
6767 Route de L'Aeroport
Saint Hubert, Quebec J3Y 8Y9

Glossary

atmosphere: the gases that surround a planet, star, or moon.

black hole: an object in space caused by the explosion and collapse of a star. This object is so tightly packed that not even light can escape the force of its gravity.

cosmic ray particles: matter from outer space. Our Sun emits some cosmic ray particles when it has large solar flares. Astronomers suspect that supernova explosions are probably responsible for many cosmic ray particles.

interstellar: between or among the stars.

light-year: the distance that light travels in one year – nearly 6 trillion miles (9.6 trillion km).

meteoroids: lumps of rock or metal drifting through space. Meteoroids can be as big as asteroids or as small as specks of dust.

orbit: the path that one celestial object or satellite follows as it circles around another object in space.

pollution: the dirtying of the air, land, water, or space.

probes: crafts that travel in space, photographing celestial bodies and even landing on some of them.

pulsars: stars with all the mass of ordinary, large stars but with that mass squeezed into a small ball. Pulsars send out rapid pulses of light or electrical waves.

quasar: the starlike core of a galaxy that may have a large black hole at its center.

radio waves: electromagnetic waves that can be detected by radio-receiving equipment.

red dwarf stars: cool, faint stars, smaller than our Sun. Red dwarfs are probably the most numerous stars in our Galaxy, but they are so faint that they are very difficult to see, even with a telescope.

satellites: smaller bodies orbiting a larger body. The Moon is Earth's natural satellite. *Sputnik 1* and *2* were Earth's first artificial satellites.

***Skylab*:** a U.S. research satellite launched in 1973. Three separate crews lived and worked on *Skylab* until 1974.

solar flares: huge explosions of intensely heated gases on the Sun that hurl out great energy. They occur near sunspots, the cooler, darker areas of the Sun.

solar wind: tiny particles that travel from the Sun's surface at a speed of about 310 miles (500 km) a second.

space shuttles: rocket ships that can be used over and over again, since they return to Earth after completing each mission.

supernova: the result of a huge star exploding. When a supernova occurs, material from the star is spread through space.

Index

Born in 1920, Isaac Asimov came to the United States as a young boy from his native Russia. As a young man, he was a student of biochemistry. In time, he became one of the most productive writers the world has ever known. His books cover a spectrum of topics, including science, history, language theory, fantasy, and science fiction. His brilliant imagination gained him the respect and admiration of adults and children alike. Sadly, Isaac Asimov died shortly after the publication of the first edition of *Isaac Asimov's Library of the Universe*.

The publishers wish to thank the following for permission to reproduce copyright material: front cover, © Pat Rawlings 1988; 4-5, 5, 6-7, Courtesy of Spacecraft Engineering Department, Naval Research Laboratory; 8, Courtesy of United States Space Command; 8-9, © Dennis Milon; 9, Courtesy of COMSAT; 10, NASA; 10-11 (upper), Courtesy of Rockwell International; 10-11 (center and lower), 12, 13, 14, 14-15, NASA; 15 (left), Courtesy of European Space Agency; 15 (right), NASA; 16-17 (upper), © Jon Pons/Courtesy of Del Woods of DayStar Filter Corporation; 16-17 (lower), Courtesy of United States Department of Energy; 17, NASA; 18, Courtesy of United States Space Command; 18-19, National Optical Astronomy Observatories; 19, NASA; 20, © David A. Hardy; 20-21 (upper), © Bruce Bond; 20-21 (lower), © David A. Hardy; 22, © Pat Rawlings 1988; 22-23, © Doug McLeod 1988; 25, © Julian Baum 1988; 26, 26-27, NASA; 27, © Adolph Schaller 1988; 29 (upper), Los Alamos National Laboratory; 29 (center), © Rick Sternbach; 29 (lower left), NASA; 29 (lower right), Mark Maxwell 1985.